Maria Tallchief

A Little Golden Book® Biography

By Patricia Morris Buckley

Illustrated by Sol Salinas

A GOLDEN BOOK • NEW YORK
Golden Books
An imprint of Random House Children's Books
A division of Penguin Random House LLC
1745 Broadway, New York, NY 10019
penguinrandomhouse.com
rhcbooks.com

Library of Congress Control Number: 2025935812
ISBN 979-8-217-11658-4 (trade) — ISBN 979-8-217-11659-1 (ebook)
Manufactured in the United States of America
10 9 8 7 6 5 4 3 2 1
EU Contact: Penguin Random House Ireland, 32 Nassau Street, Dublin D02 YH68.
https://eu-contact.penguin.ie

Elizabeth Marie Tall Chief was born on January 24, 1925, on the Osage Reservation in Fairfax, Oklahoma. Her father was an Osage Native. Her mother was Scottish and Irish. She had an older brother, Jerry, and a younger sister, Marjorie. Her family called her Betty Marie.

No one could have dreamed that she, a Native American girl from the prairies, would one day become a famous ballerina, performing on stages all over the world!

Betty Marie took her first ballet class when she was just three years old. Her mother had wanted to dance when she was growing up in Kansas, but her family couldn't afford to pay for lessons. She was happy that her girls could study dance and piano. Oil had been found on the Osage Reservation, making the people of the tribe wealthy.

Betty Marie loved music and dance. She woke up an hour early every day to practice piano and spent hours after school in dance classes. Soon, the sisters were performing together at fairs and rodeos around Oklahoma.

One of Betty Marie's favorite childhood memories was when her grandmother took her and Marjorie to watch Osage dancing on the reservation. This was done in secret because Native customs, like dancing, had been outlawed by the United States government.

According to Osage tradition, only men could dance. They dressed in blankets, beads, and pants with bells. The *thunk, thunk, thunk* of the beating drums stayed with Betty Marie all her life.

When Betty Marie turned eight, her family moved to Los Angeles, California, where there were more opportunities for the girls to study dance. Their parents enrolled the sisters at Ernest Belcher's dancing school. Even though they had taken lessons for years, Mr. Belcher told them that they hadn't been taught proper foot placements and leg positions. The girls would have to start over in the beginner class!

The sisters worked hard to catch up, spending long hours at the ballet school. They were just as devoted to the piano and practiced every day.

Betty Marie had perfect pitch. This meant she could hear a note and then play it accurately on the piano. Her mother dreamed of her one day becoming a concert pianist.

As a new student, she had a hard time making friends at school. Some of the other children bullied Betty Marie. They laughed at her last name, asking her if it was "Tall" or "Chief." She decided to combine them into one word: Tallchief.

When Betty Marie turned twelve, she began studying at the dance school of Bronislava Nijinska. Madame Nijinska was a former ballerina and a choreographer, someone who directs the dance movements for ballets. She was a strict teacher who demanded perfection.

Betty Marie loved listening to the music and making it come to life with her dancing. Soon, she quit piano to focus on dance. With ballet, she would have both movement *and* music.

Madame Nijinska choreographed several ballets at a famous outdoor theater called the Hollywood Bowl. Betty Marie was disappointed when she learned she would be in the corps de ballet, a group of background dancers. Her mother encouraged her to do her best no matter how small her part was. When Madame Nijinska saw how hard Betty Marie worked, she moved her up to a lead role in another production.

After graduating from high school in 1942, Betty Marie started dancing professionally. Her first job was as a background dancer in the film *Presenting Lily Mars,* starring the famous actress Judy Garland. But Betty Marie didn't enjoy dancing in movies—she found the routines too simple. When another ballerina invited her to go to New York City to take dance lessons, she jumped at the chance.

While in New York, seventeen-year-old Betty Marie auditioned for the Ballet Russe de Monte Carlo, a well-known ballet company. A few days later, a space opened up for a new dancer—and the Ballet Russe offered her a job!

Betty Marie started out dancing small parts, but she quickly moved on to larger roles.

The head of Ballet Russe suggested Betty Marie change her last name to a Russian-sounding one. Many American dancers did this at the time, because the most famous ballerinas were from Russia. But Betty Marie refused, determined to keep her Osage identity. She did decide to drop "Betty Marie" and go by the more formal "Maria." From then on, people knew her as Maria Tallchief.

At Ballet Russe, Maria worked with the famous choreographer George Balanchine. Impressed by Maria's abilities, he helped her stretch further and jump higher.

Maria and George grew close while working together and married on August 16, 1946.

Two years later, George helped start the New York City Ballet. Maria soon joined him there.

Audiences and critics loved seeing her dance the lead roles in famous ballets that George choreographed, like *The Firebird, Swan Lake,* and *The Nutcracker.* Maria became the New York City Ballet's first prima ballerina—or top female dancer—and the first American and Native American prima ballerina in the world!

Maria and George eventually ended their marriage, but they continued to work together and remained good friends.

A few years later, she found love again. She married Henry "Buzz" Paschen, a businessman from Chicago, and had a daughter named Elise.

At the age of forty-one, Maria retired from professional dancing to spend more time with her family. She taught ballet for twenty years and founded the Chicago City Ballet with her sister, Marjorie, who was also a successful ballerina.

For her many accomplishments as a ballerina, Maria was inducted into the National Women's Hall of Fame and received a Kennedy Center Honor. She was awarded the National Medal of Arts by President Bill Clinton. Her image appeared on both a United States dollar coin and a quarter. There was even a Barbie doll made to look like her!

But Maria's greatest honor was receiving a new title by the Osage Tribal Council. She was given the name Wa-Xthe-Thonba, Osage for "Woman of Two Worlds." Maria was proud to be both a famous ballerina and part of the Osage nation.

Maria Tallchief died on April 11, 2013. She is remembered not only as an elegant, athletic dancer but also as the first American and Native American prima ballerina. She danced for audiences around the world and showed that, with hard work and dedication, anyone can reach great heights!